# Spring Song

## from *Love's Labour's Lost*
## by William Shakespeare

WHEN daizies pied, and violets blue,

And lady-smocks all silver-white,

And cuckoo-buds of yellow hue,

4

Do paint the meadows with delight,

The cuckoo then, on every tree,

Mocks marry'd men,
for thus sings he, Cuckoo;

7

Cuckoo, cuckoo,
– O word of fear,
Unpleasing to a married ear!

8

WHEN shepherds pipe on oaten straws

And merry larks are plowmen's clocks,

When turtles tread, and rooks, and daws,

And maidens bleach their summer smocks

The cuckoo then, on every tree,

Mocks married men,
for thus sings he,
Cuckoo;

Cuckoo, cuckoo, – O word of fear,
Unpleasing to a marry'd ear!

Two Rivers Press 1997:
illustrations by Peter Hay;
lettering by Pip Hall.
Reprinted 2005